G000095207

the JOY
of BEING
YOU

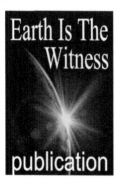

Earth Is The
Witness

publication

the JOY

of BEING

YOU

*an illuminating
discovery of who YOU are*

Petar Umiljanovic

Earth Is The Witness publication

ISBN 9798366774475

Thank You for Your Contribution !

Cover design by
Petar Umiljanovic

Earth Is The Witness

This is my Intellect
my Heart & Soul

speaking to You
in words of
Infinite Consciousness

my endless Love
for this World

for You

As You read it through

it will reward You
being forever written in
the Universe's Book of Life

I LOVE YOU

Contents

Contents ... 7
INTRODUCTION ... 9

Y<u>OU</u> (who you are?) ... **18**

(what you are?) **<u>the BEING</u>** ... **44**

<u>of JOY</u> (you are!) ... **78**

About the Author ... 109

to Angie,
for all your love...

INTRODUCTION

Welcome, Dear Reader!

I need to be alone somewhere, more often, so that I can comprehend existence with clear consciousness. I know it is the purpose of my life.

So I have set out there to experience the basics, just me in nature, to start writing from that fundament.

It is the force of presentness, a direct

experience of our true basic nature.

In our previous book:
CONSCIOUSNESS & The WORLD
– Narrations of AWAKENING :
UNIVERSAL WISDOM FOR SPIRITUAL
ENLIGHTENMENT, we have mainly focused
on general, universal, and global aspects of
consciousness.

If you haven't read it, I strongly encourage
and recommend you to do, as it is undeniably
linked to this one.

First, here is a summary of its ten chapters:

- The book follows the story of existence
itself, thus, in the first chapter, we address the
basic existential questions of Self-awareness,
consciousness, God, and how mind and matter
are created within such engagement of
beingness in itself.

- Then, somewhat similar to the Carl Sagan
Cosmos spaceship of imagination, we will fly
through the universe, within the beautiful
vastness of space, to attain the sense of
material existence.

- As we arrive on the earth, our story will be

of the human soul, looking at the awesome, original ambience of life, thus reminding the reader of who we were, are, and can be again.

- Conversely, we next dive deeply into the whole illusion of separation within modern civilisation whilst offering spiritual and practical methods of staying present and healthy.

- This newfound strength will take us travelling on a journey where we will enjoy and experience the full spectrum of human culture, history, and adventure.

- Such profound insights push us deeper into the Self, and we'll start to let go of worldly attachments as we start relaxing our minds and egos.

- In seeing the light of ourselves, we will awaken to the true Self, consciousness, thus further unveiling illusions.

- By abiding in the awakening, we shall return to the bliss of nature, free from civilisation, prevailing in natural time and space.

- That fundamental connection to the environment will have a lasting effect on our awareness, and we will explore its many insights through our understanding of pure consciousness.

- Finally, all these experiences, realisations,

and this wisdom will be reflected by looking at the current situation in the world, offering inspiring personal change and widespread global action!

In this book, however, we will dive into the close and personal experience of self-awareness. We will directly enter the holy ground of our light Being, which in its essence, is pure undulated Joy. That is the real truth of **who** and **what** YOU are.

Here, I will help you to awaken to that power inside you that has been patiently waiting to be fully realised and lived in accordance with your true life's purpose.

That purpose is as simple, natural, and light as the very consciousness that you, me, and all the beings in the universe are. This consciousness is the present background from which entire existence is derived and to which it will ultimately return.

And this booklet is another undertaking of conscious wisdom for spiritual enlightenment.

It is a deeply awakening work of inspirational beauty, with a strong and confident voice directly addressing the reader.

The idea for these books is to document the most fundamental story of human and conscious existence.

We are all on a spiritual and existential journey from a young age, and for me that depth of discovery has resulted in the insights I'm sharing with You here.

Consciousness is fundamental to existence, and I have written about it from many angles and reflections as an honest and open message to humanity.

So these books address the problem of personal and collective unconsciousness, which has resulted in the growing social, economic, and environmental crisis.

The solutions are: becoming fully conscious of ourselves, going back to nature, and taking sustainable action.

The key inspirational point here is the as yet unseen conscious clarity and spiritual inspiration that lies within the realism of staying present. As the reader goes through the story of awakening, they will behold a refreshing new approach to non-duality, alongside the sense of a complete existential picture. These unquestionable depths of personal experience, have been beautifully written to capture attention, deeply move, and awaken joy.

I most sincerely invite You to openly receive this message, to willingly enter the atmosphere of your aware Being, to feel this innate Joy, and benefit from its basic but most profound, awakening wisdom.

As You support me, You help me to continue working on these books. As such, we together, can ensure that this message will reach humanity to inspire personal and global well-being for a sustainable future!

I invite YOU, dear Soul, to join me in yet another journey of self-discovery.

For this, we are destined and meant to be...

I'm wishing you to be
the best person always;

original, healthy, inspired

I'm wishing you to be the
best sibling, friend, relative,
partner, parent, and teacher

to follow your intuition,
insights, dreams, imagination

to feel the entire humanity,
nature, earth, and the
universe as yourself

to feel at home
anywhere you are

I'm wishing you
a happy new

You

CHAPTER 1

YOU

(who you are?)

INVITATION

The remnants of the vivid past are still etched in my consciousness, like glimpses of the once-forgotten present. The future holds anguish obscured by memories that are destined to repeat.

One does not escape what his soul has yearned for; the authenticity of the loneliest despair and the freedom to suffer unto myself. What is life but succumbing to the inevitability of one's hopelessness, unwillingness, and losing yourself in pointlessness?

Emptiness is real, isolation deadly. The joy inside is all but forgotten. The world is real, so real, and unfriendly. Nervous boredom is now a common sight, the only friend is paper, and the only tool is a pen.

What is the point of such existence other than to dwell deeper into the meaninglessness of it all? The excitement of waiting for death to save me from the blatant ignorance towards the earth being paradise itself makes life a living hell.

But I can not see it anymore. I can not feel it for what it is. Like a lost sense, I'm robbed of life's joy, of the pleasantness of being. I must go to nature again. I must stop dwelling on the pain that is robbing me of my life energy.

Are you tired of feeling like that? Are you tired of fake spirituality? Do you want to discover who and what You are?

I can show you how to access that
knowledge very quickly and simply.
You don't have to trust me unquestioningly,
since your personal authentic experience
will open up the self-inquiry within you,
independently initiating you on your
own journey of self-discovery.

The great book is like a good song.
The more you listen to it, the better it becomes,
as it better and better begins to sound.

In this booklet of spiritual wisdom based
on the topic of consciousness, I'll show you
reality. You will simply need to open your
mind and your heart, then invite
the depth of your soul.

But first sit, relax, and breathe!

WHO ARE YOU?

Here is the quickest way to find
the freedom of knowing yourself:

Break away from your comfort zone. Go
out to nature alone for an entire day. Observe
yourself, your thoughts, and your feelings.

Notice how you feel being free like that in nature. Imagine being out tHere for an entire lifetime. Would you miss anything, or would you feel free and fulfilled? Would you lose yourself or discover more of who you are?

You have to strip yourself down like that, methodically extract from an entire world. You have to be free from the system, emancipated at least for a day, to allow more presence into your awareness. Be a mindful individual. Independent and comfortable alone.

Look at the tree, stay close to it, and feel the raw nature of its existence as plant life. Imagine how it is to be soil, grass, tree, insect, animal, or light, which is everywhere, as consciousness.

Take long deep breaths while being fully aware of them. Touch the grass, trees, and water. Feel the wind and disappear into the atmosphere of natural vastness.

Be as wide as the horizon, open like the sky, yet close to the Self like the ground that's stuck to your feet. Be an entire globe, be the world, as consciousness. Feel the expansion of your mind and be the present centre of it.

You know no boundaries; you are limitless. You are timeless. You hold every moment dear; you are infinite. You treasure every being; you are kindness itself. You can remain motionless like this, yet you have travelled everywhere. You are always alone, even when accompanied by the entire universe of silence whilst surrounded by the masses.

You abide in that sacred silence, for in its peace is where you dwell in knowledge, and attain wisdom. Would you ignore all that and shut down the door of universal insight, the eternal truth?

Now you know that it always patiently lies within you, inside you, you know that it is You. Providing you allow it to be as it IS.

Undisturbed, unbroken. Aware, constant, loving. That is You. The Joy of Being. The Being of Joy.

Love that, love yourself.

I love myself.

I Love YOU!

DO YOU?

Freedom from yourself, your problems,
is YOU, the JOY.

When we say You, it implies something
personal, involving you as a person, a character, and the story of your life. But what is this
You really? Do you know who You are?
Can you know what You are? Maybe you will
think about your gender, age, social status,
career, religion, and beliefs first; all the obvious
aspects of identity. On this level, every person
would tell a different story.

The world is filled with countless destinies
that we associate with and like to tell each
other. Most human conversations, books,
movies, etc., revolve around sharing personal
experiences. It seems we have identified with
these stories to the point where, on the whole,
they rule, influence, and determine
the course of our lives.

You are none of these stories. You can
not be found in ideas, words, thoughts, or
stereotypes. You are the very knowing of any
such experience, the awareness that observes
stories, ideas, and perceptions, which can not

be put into past or future context as you are the constancy of being conscious. Whereby allowing the world to freely pass you through the senses, you remain in the power of now, like a magnet of natural awareness keeping you centred in presence.

Once you learn to recognise your natural state through observing all the passing states, you will love them all. You will love yourself in any form and idea you might appear to yourself, for in the free observance there is no judgment.

In this holy mercy of staying in grace, you are free from yourself. Then, you will understand and know deep in your being what it means to be consciousness, the living spirit of wisdom, observing the current experience of reality.

This state of pure perception is mindfulness. That is the closest truth of YOU that I or anyone else can point you to. It is the simplest form of knowing, but it is devoid of knowledge. It is the present recognition of what is, but it is nothing. It is natural focus, but it is effortless.

It is the awareness of happenings, the silence, that which remains.

Meditation is a legitimate technique for inviting or fostering awareness; through sufficient observance of an unsettled mind, it will become your constant state. It will be you, in which you recognise yourself as the aware Self that you are.

This simplicity of unseparated feeling is what we call Non-duality. A natural perception of reality through the one true Self.

With meditation, you can eliminate the things you don't really need in life, like addictions. Thus, it is like an investment towards attaining freedom.

This freedom from needs and pleasures is the foremost prerequisite for achieving awakening, which is now, in every conscious breath, for which there is no need to lose it. Find satisfaction in inner peace and, in turn, you will find yourself.

If you want to feel better about your life situation immediately, know that, sadly, one billion people live in poverty as we speak, and 25,000 people die from hunger every day. You are lucky to live in a somewhat free part of the world, to have a job, safety, and food.

ARE YOU AWARE?

People tend to say that life is short.
But life is not short, it is long, especially when
you are aware of it. Moments can seem like an
eternity, which consciousness is; an eternity
in a moment. Even more so if you often find
yourself alone or lack a career to occupy
most of your time.

If you find yourself isolated and idle, life
will be an eternity for you, and you will not
want or need more or less of it, it will just
be exactly as it is.

Time and thought are interrelated and,
with self-awareness, you will not perceive
either. The moment will be eternal and
space will feel miraculous, thus inducing
the universal recognition of appreciation
for this blessing of being that we call god.

You are the most sacred awareness of the
miracle of life. You are the life itself, the one
consciousness expressed in experience as a
human being, the divine being according
to the oneness of existence.

The main reason people say that life is

short is that they miss most of it, so they feel sorry for not living it while it has lasted.

Most people live simple household lives, in a state of perpetual waiting. What are they waiting for?

They, as kids, are waiting for friends to come over and play. Waiting to go to kindergarten and for school to finish. Waiting on parents to take them to their favourite place or buy the toy they have wanted and waited to obtain for so long. Waiting for that boy/girl to finally like us and return the sympathies.

Then they wait for the so-called proper job and career, for the right partner, to start a family. Waiting to build, buy or rent a house. Waiting for their partners to come home from work, for their children to be born and, once arrived, waiting for them to grow up.

People are waiting for the clubs they support to win the title or the league, for their country's team to win the tournament or the World Cup. And some are waiting for their countries to become independent.

People are waiting for the prophets and their god to appear. Finally, they are waiting for their retirement and death.

We are all waiting for a better life, for civilisation to progress, to save itself and the planet.

Humanity is in a state of waiting and doing, but life is too short for that.

What we are missing is Being. The pure presence of awareness. The timeless Beingness.

The Being is the light, the Joy of who and what You are. We carry this light forever inside. Even when unaware of it, it is tHere underneath the thought. THere, before reaction, before losing oneself in the world.

The light is the sanity of awareness, the peace of presence. It is your authentic point of view, as the soul that is taking you on the experience of universality on earth. The soul that you are is the being of light, connection with one spirit, god, and consciousness.

You are born to experience the particular lifestyle that your soul needs to learn, grow, remember, and return to the primal and eternal home as the singularity of all that IS.

There are 8 billion human souls on this planet, and probably infinite others in the universe, multiverse, and beyond, so your characteristic flavour of sanity is the richness and the beauty of separation that you are destined to awaken from.

Awakening will bring tears of joy to your heart, soul, and face. This recognition can only come with the presence, inseparable from your awareness of breath, constantly and absolutely, acquainted and no stranger to the warmth in your heart.

Your body is therefore relaxed, forehead smooth, eyes focused, smile gentle, awareness present. Breath can flow long and deep until it disappears in the concentrated but fully tranquil centre.

You should feel this; feel it, be it.

**You are Joy, You are Light,
You are Consciousness**

OBSERVE YOUR REACTIONS

Can you feel the relaxation, the lightness?
Do you feel the joy of yourself, the Joy of YOU?
Are you enjoying this illuminating journey of
discovering who you are? Does it feel pleasant,
free, awakening, liberating, enlightening?
Have you managed to envision the freedom
that I'm describing here? Can you feel it?
Are you it?

Does it feel exciting or peaceful? Are you
able to notice the layers of resistance and are
they naturally falling off? Can you be naked,
innocent, honest, and accepting in
the face of these truths?

Does it hurt? Is it inviting or boring?
Do you feel like losing, gaining, or being
at peace with it? Do you feel at home or in
a strange land or space? Is it helpful, do you
want to share it with others? Can you live
with it, are you afraid of it?

Does this recognition of your true self settle
you in an unexplainable peace, does it manifest
bliss in you? Does it feel graceful and loving,
or irritatingly aggregating? Do you care,
or couldn't care less?

Notice how your thoughts, feelings, and perceptions react to this information. Follow it with awareness. Is there any shame, pride, self-importance, rejection, or anger in you?

Notice who reacts, who feels provoked or bored? Informed or misinformed? Follow any movement of thought in you, any judgment. Trace it back to the source of sensation, to the belief in your false self-identity. To the pre-established notions of your patterns of behaviour. To the belief that you are a predetermined character identified by certain ideas, positions in life, beliefs, associations, belongings, and investments. If you're holding on to identity you're holding on to ideas.

So do you hold on to anything, anything at all? Do you see the freedom in holding on to nothing, in embracing emptiness? Do you take God to be a suppression or celebration of life and yourself?

See, you are not separate from God. How could you be? God is the conscious essence. You are consciousness, a god that is the Self. And there is no false sense of self. We can only talk about the length of certain selves, and in

that investigation find out which are lasting,
ever-present, and eternal.

Create no more separation by waiting
or wanting anything outside of yourself.
The only absolute joy is your natural being.
That is where you will find yourself.
That is where the joy resides.
That is you, it is all in you,
and you are it.
You are everything; all of that, all of it.
There is no other than this Self.

There is a conscious being looking
through your eyes. A being that is being
aware. A recognition of the senses.
An observation of presentness.
That being feels itself as kindness
and knows itself as stillness.

Know your being as such a presence
of awareness. Feel it realised in your heart
deeply and you will carry its blessings
throughout your life and more.
You are a being of joy, light,
and consciousness.

RELATIONSHIPS

People who are mature and know what life is will always be nice, respectful, and never hurt you. With open hearts and minds, they care only about others feeling good and sharing that inspiration.

All the people who hurt you in the past simply were not mature enough. Actually, there is no reason to feel hurt, for they themselves are victims of their ego. There is nothing personal about this, it is only a matter of their own personality getting the better of them.

There are billions of people in the world but not many have open hearts and souls. That is something you need to create for yourself to have a life truly worth living.

The law of attraction is a double sided mirror. And just like the sun is always shining and never looks back in introspection questioning its worth, you need to align with your light source essence, consciousness. Be the mirror that is only pointing out, radiating with the power of your unconditional love's luminosity.

The fact that you are conscious is the reason why you are different to people around you.

You are aware of yourself, while others are asleep. But you can listen to your thoughts and observe your feelings because you are free, which is why you are neither fully lost in tradition nor modernity. To become genuine you only need to recognise the wisdom that this freedom brings.

With this understanding let us now look at some different types of relationships.

To have a true soul partner is the most important value we can have in life. No matter who we are, the right partner will always uplift our life to a new level. But if it comes from the selfishness of ego, romantic love can spiral into madness. Love and hate are the two sides of the same ego. One is possessive, addictive, and manipulatory, while the other is irritative, repulsive, and aversive. Both are based on a dualistic perception of the world and a strong sense of clinging to individuality.

Unconditional love doesn't want anything so it doesn't seek anything for itself. She is pure consciousness, for which reason mystics don't have partners, they already abide in the pure state and their essential nature. Romantic love shouldn't be the basis of a relationship, consciousness should. It means peace, the home to which you return and feel either in yourself or in your partner.

This peace is not subject to circumstances, time, or life situations. With the right partner, a relationship that is based on such timeless values of love will endure until old age.

But first, consider your relationship with your parents.

How do you feel about them? On their very mention do you feel happy, about them, for them, or because of them? Does knowing about them bring joy or pain to your heart? Are they your weak spot or something to be proud of? Do you contact them often, and how often do you see them? Can you openly talk to them about any subject, or do you rather avoid raising any issue around them? If they have passed away, do you feel sad or relieved?

And what about other members of
your family? How do you feel about them?
Your siblings, relatives, and grandparents?
Is there any tension between you?

And friends? Are they really your true
friends or people you just happen to know
and hang out with? Would you rather not see
or stay in contact with them, or do they still
bring you social and general value? Can you
be absolutely open with any of these people?
When is the last time you had a meaningful
conversation? When and with whom did you
have the best one? Do you still have to dream
about having a true, genuine friendship?

And what about your career and hobbies?
Do you have either? Do you like your job; do
you live and work the life of your dreams?
Are you a leader in constant progress or just
an everyday worker? Do you want to spend
your life working and living like that?
What are you going to do about this?
Are you working hard on accomplishing all of
the above, or are you working hard to survive
and make ends meet, just going by, like most
of humanity? If you can't wait to go home from

work, or if you can't wait to leave home to go to work, you still have work to do on yourself.

The highest joy you can achieve is pursuing your destined career, your innermost purpose in life, for that is to awaken who you truly are.

This brings us to the final question.
How is the relationship with your partner going? Is it a romantic relationship where you enjoy telling them how much you love them? Are you over the moon with it or wishing you had never met them? What are the reasons that keep you motivated to continue it? Are you in love with them, or just infatuated and afraid of being alone?

And what about your kids, do you spend enough quality time with them? Are you proud of them, and are you their best friend or in constant conflict? Are you the same person with or without them?

Have you found your true unchanging, eternal nature? One that is centred in the timeless awareness of being rather than subject to influence from life situations? Can you hold that loving frequency throughout the day and your lifetime?

In the end, the only true relationship you will ever have, the only one that matters, is the one you have with yourself. How deeply you know yourself as consciousness will determine how you behave with others.

From wherever you draw your sense of worth and belonging, such an investment will meet an eventual demise. Or in other words, you will suffer from any attachment. Loving too much will eventually hurt a lot.

Instead, align yourself with everlasting awareness and set up your relationships based on that unshakable power of presence. This will keep you centred in the moment, where every interaction will be free and open just like the infinite space that you are.

To give you an example of how powerful this true freedom is, consider Buddha. He loved his family immensely, but once he felt the need to find that deeper truth of himself, he left them, and the rest changed history.

This does not mean you shouldn't love, rather, it means you should not be a victim of fears and desires. You finally have the courage to act on your highest enthusiasm and follow your deepest intuition.

It is in such freedom that only true unconditional love can flourish and withstand any situation that life will inevitably throw at you. You will not be seeking and clinging to love, attention, and pleasure, but sharing your natural joy of being, which is inexhaustible and unconditional. You don't stay in a separation mindset, you abide in the true universal freedom of infinite space of awareness, and you act according to the endless possibilities that being free provides.

Embody this truth and invite the treasures of unlimited inner knowledge, of which the greatest is your capacity to care, cherish, and embrace all living creatures in their natural form and state.

You only have your illusions to lose.

YOU

To conclude this chapter, we will make a simple observation of us, that is You, in life.

If you want to live the authentic free life,

the dream you are born to envisage and manifest, you have to eventually discover who you truly are. This happens by investigating the nature of who and what you think you are now. By diving deep down to the basis of reality, your true self will be known.

We have looked into several ways to practice or inspire such inner, personal observation, however, the most popular method is meditation.

Meditation can be practised, performed, and observed anywhere. It is not necessary to do it strictly anywhere in particular, be it in nature, a silent, dark, or light room, as these environmental factors shouldn't affect our awareness of being. Nevertheless, for the purpose of this particular illuminating transmission, I decided to focus on the sunshine and light aspect of existence, as it is the external option that is closest and most related to life.

I enjoy that warm sensation so much that it changes my attitude towards spiritual or meditative stereotypes, and it gives me the courage to completely follow my own best inspiration of illuminating light.

But first, try the situation that works best for you, which is probably just being where you are most comfortable, perhaps, your living room or bedroom. Upon sitting still with your body fully relaxed, something will begin to happen. You may notice a lot of tension begin to bother you. You may find it very uncomfortable, boring, or even pointless.

If this is your first taste of meditation, it will be one of the strangest experiences you have gotten yourself into.

Something so simple as trying to sit still is proving to be the most difficult thing in the world. And that is a good start, so don't worry about it. The important thing is that you decide to stick with it for a couple of weeks, much like going on a diet.

Now, you've been trying these sitting-still sessions for a couple of days, and even though there is not much obvious progress yet, now you know what you are up against. Your mind and body are not under your possession. You are unable to control yourself, and this realisation is the main progress! You have glimpsed how your character has been in charge of your life up until now, but you now notice that there is another you who is aware of this other you, mainly of your unconscious traits, personality, bodily sensations, and urges.

By realising how we are consciously aware of our many personalities, we start working on our true character, which is our soul.

And the soul is wise, loving, eternal.

Life is a dream of the Soul

To know that you are a sacred soul requires meditation and self-reflection, the inner experience and recognition of thoughts, feelings, sensations, and perceptions.

This new you, you now know is unnamable, timeless, formless, always alive, or better say, awake. The New You that is now awakening was always here, you now know, and it is your natural awareness of being.

I Am home
with You

we are the light
of this world

I don't have to
accomplish anything
else to be home

as I Am
with You

and all else is a
blissful bonus

I Am home
in the union
with God

with You

I Am

(what you are?)

the BEING

INVITATION

Let's revisit our back-cover inspiration!

The authenticity of your soul – the original feeling and experience of it is the best teacher in life. To absolutely understand what I'm

pointing towards here, it is crucial that
you try this the way I present it below:

Go out to your garden or nearby park
and walk barefoot on the grass, enjoying the
freedom and freshness of the most natural
of sensations in such a simple act.
Lay on the grass, keep looking at the sky as
you are bathed by the sun; feel the pull of the
moment, ignite your inner flame, and stay
in abiding grace.

Then close your eyes and take in a deep
breath of that warm, orange, radiant sunshine.
That's where we come from; that is our home.
Without this luminosity, there is no life.
You are such a being of light!

This light is not an idea, symbolism, or
some abstract spiritual concept; it is who you
are in essence. Even in science today, we have
begun to acknowledge the fact that we are
pure consciousness. We are the light out of
and in which the entire universe appears.

Knowing this for yourself, as the sacred
presence of awareness, will open up the
natural flow of your life.

You have to feel it for yourself;
the sensation of warmth, the colours, the
texture of the ground beneath your bare feet.
Your body's skin as you're lying down.

Relax into the moment of being this
experience. Fully immersed yourself in the
atmosphere of freedom and the pleasantness
of warmth. Feel how you are united with the
earth, sun, and universe. Never separate. You
are atomic, chemical, and biological extensions
of them. You are the pure consciousness that
knows and feels this unity with the elements
of light. You are being life.

The oneness That IS.

The bliss of feeling complete.

the JOY of BEING YOU.

**You are a powerful being of light
that knows no fear and embodies
divine intelligence**

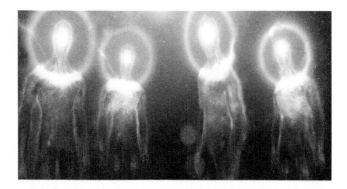

Isn't this the best feeling ever? Isn't this like being at your true home? Is there anything else you want? What else could you possibly want? Isn't this who you are? Being free like that. Being free, at last.

Knowing that this sensation is where you have come from and where you will go, before birth, after the death of imagination.

See, we spend an entire life imagining something else, dreaming about the afterlife, wondering about the birth of time. Wanting to be something that we are not. Hence the search. And our destiny in this life is largely determined by such aggravations. We have missed the most obvious truth, the simplest answer, the secret of what we are...

LIGHT

The essential appearance of the universe is black. The visible light is mere dust in the ocean of darkness, but for us biological beings, there is no life without light, without the sun. We are drifting on the surface of one speck of matter in this endless sea of dark.

How can we then say that what we essentially are is the light of consciousness, *the light of the world?*

The brain receives electrical impulses from the five senses, and the mind creates a representation of that as vision. But this vision is dreamed in the dark cranium of the skull, inside the brain. It is not really out there as such. Consciousness is the light by which we seem to be able to see, that is, to imagine, to dream this apparent solid reality.

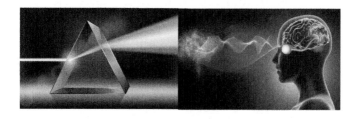

Consciousness is neither black nor white, but by associating with the light, with the sun, which is eternal from our standpoint and is essential for life, we are justifyingly inspiring ourselves to get closer to home. We breathe sighs of relief as we escape from the travesty of the current situation: the status quo.

The deep states of meditation, as well as near-death experiences or religious visions are

most often described as the white light.
This is what I mean by us being the light.

We must presume that these experiences
and visions occur when stripped of the five
senses and are perceived in their pure state,
which we call light. And this light is the same
throughout existence. It is universal,
it is consciousness.

So whether we are looking at ourselves as
being the light as an inspiration or as the literal
reality, either is true and useful. Except for the
illusion that we are already experiencing,
what other possibility is there?

This illuminating nature of our true being
is how it feels to be awakened, as it is as light
as the light itself. Knowing this in your awareness, feeling this in your heart, and being this
as you are is enlightenment. That is who we
are, not as some extraordinary achievement,
but simply relaxing the perceptions into the
peaceful aura of our loving being.

We can track the light in every aspect
of reality, and the sun is the most relative
and obvious one.

MYSTERY OF THE SUN

There is no question that the sun is the oldest and most widely used depiction of existence, life, wisdom, illumination, and awakening there is.

Ancient people have been aligning their monuments with the sun, moon, and stars since the beginning of organised society.

Those places are still truly mysterious and mythical, for they have the sky and soul embedded within them, successfully captivating humanity for thousands of years.

Many cultures indulged in sun worship, thus many religions and hundreds of deities bore shapes, marks, meanings, and symbolism based on these celestial objects. These deities are attributed and associated with the sun's influence and the effects of its energy.

Egyptians worshipped the sun god Ra, representing life (ankh), power, energy, warmth, and growth.

The Inca's version of the sun god is Inti.

Apollo is the Greek one, as well as Helios that proudly stood as the Colossus of Rhodes, from which the sun crown on the Statue of Liberty is derived.

This is an understandable relationship, similar to how we appreciate our parents and grandparents for giving us life, most cultures use some form of solar motifs.

Even today, it is still probably the most frequently used symbol in company logos and is most often associated with secret societies and Illuminati.

The sun is the burning behind the all-seeing eye, with which they have aligned themselves for the obvious reason of receiving light energy as it provides us with benevolent conditions for life.

We will not go into the depths of physics here, as there is still so much left to discover on the nature of electromagnetism and radiation. But let's just say that the sun is a ball of plasma or liquid magma powered

by a nuclear fusion reaction in its centre,
or it is some sort of a portal.

Whatever it may be, it emanates photons
as basic pockets of light. We will only look at
that basic relationship of these universal forces
and energies that are at the source of life
phenomena here on earth (and probably
everywhere else in the universe).

We are a part of the universal chain
reaction of transmitted energy. And although
everything literally exists only as a dream in
consciousness, we can establish and measure
some laws and predictions, for the dream
seems so long and solid that we call it a reality.

In this reality, we can notice and compare
the patterns of consciousness in the behaviour
of light, therefore confidently using this
obvious correlation to further our spiritual
understanding and illuminate ourselves
towards enlightenment.

If we look at the beginning of the universe,
we trace it back to the Big Bang, the singularity
of all illusory mass, the point of consciousness,
and oneness. And it is irrelevant here whether

God is responsible or is a part of this existential link of life, as he can not be the fundament. That consciousness IS.

This dreamed mass in consciousness has expanded into the visible spectrum of light and is invisible as radiation. All of this has a direct effect on the earth, on biological, and to some degree, possibly even on spiritual beings.

The sun emits solar radiation, which once again includes visible and ultraviolet light, infrared, radio waves, X-rays, and gamma rays. These energies are simply heat or thermal radiation from the sun that we feel as warmth.

Mass or energy is always vibrating, therefore it is always in motion. This interconnected movement of particles and radiation in the universe, the yin and yang, act in certain patterns, like the spin of torus flow, which gives shapes to galaxies, suns, and solar systems.

 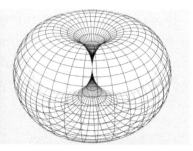

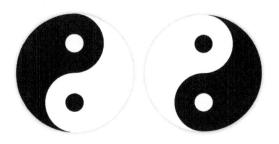

Human chakras are clearly such spins too as wheels of light, anchoring certain bodily functions in the physical plexus of the soul. They are the root signature of our divine being, expressed in the matter as energy points of human life. They are holy centres of living essence spinning the soul charm into manifested existence as a living, breathing, speaking, interacting, sensing, procreating, illuminating, feeling, growing, and tasting biological being.

Even the human body emits biophotons from its own energy field or aura.

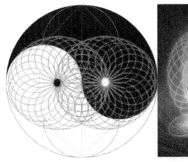

These are links to our soul essence, keeping the mystery of existence fully experienced through its conscious channels. Thus, you are the centre of this mystery, which performs its magical, healing, refreshing, and blissful energies within you as the natural joy of your being.

We can also observe this rotating movement on the universal scale, in nature here on earth as a fractal pattern of the Mandelbrot set.

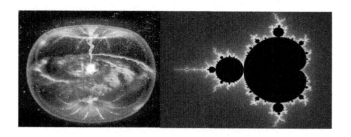

Earth's geology and biology are influenced and shaped by its universal pulsating wake.

The rivers and trees; the vegetable, fruits and flowers; the weather and climate all play in this swirling, growing motion.

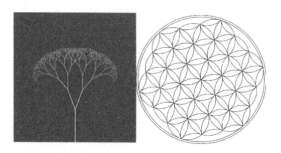

And for us on earth, the sun is the most important link and connection to life.

We are now a self-conscious part of the long process of energetic motion, one which results in the assembly or creation of molecules and biological cells for both animal and plant organisms. The sun's light is essential for human health; we require the sun's energy to live and survive, directly through heat and indirectly through food.

It generates the production of vitamin D, the most important of the vitamins due to its role in many bodily functions.

Sunlight can benefit the human body in the following ways: support better sleep, uplift your mood, fight off depression, increase energy, improve symptoms of mental health conditions, lower blood pressure, lower the risk of metabolic syndrome, heal inflammation, prevent cancer, strengthen bones, keep off excess weight, extend life expectancy, and uplift you spiritually.

Many animals, those referred to as cold-blooded, can't even function without first heating themselves in the sun. While mammals and other groups possess the privilege of warm blood, we all depend on the sun's energy in the form of heat or food.

Yet another crucial relationship with the sun is the process of photosynthesis through which plant and plankton life generate their energy and food. As a byproduct, they release oxygen which we depend on to develop as biological animals and, furthermore, as self-aware beings.

It is of utmost importance for you to tap into the sun's energy that's harnessed in fruits and vegetables for natural healing and benefits to your well-being. Followed with regular exercise and outdoor activities to breathe life into you.

Without the sun there is no life; it gives us life similar to an all-loving god. But akin to the wrath of God, just a slight change in the earth's climate or a solar burst could kill us. We are at the mercy of its glowing longevity cycles.

Still, both in mythology and reality, the sun defeats darkness over and over again, until eventually, we all return to the everlasting light as consciousness.

It is clear how the sun has been bestowed its god-like status, its deity identity, as it literally is our natural god.

So there is no doubt that the sun is the most important link in the story of life on earth. Feeling, understanding, and appreciating this direct truth is our spiritual and conscious connection to it.

We as consciousness are the light of this world, and the sun's light is the visible and sensible correlation and counterpart in this relationship where the physical world is dreamed in consciousness.

I have no doubt that even without scientific understanding, ancient people have felt and known the importance of sun light, and have delved deep into this mystery by intuitively practising the spiritual correlations of its life-giving properties in the form of solar yoga.

SUNGAZING

The most common choice of vacation or holiday entails bathing in the sea and soaking up in the sun. Although unaware of how or why, they feel the benefits of both, people are attracted to their therapeutic and mental healing effects.

Many people ignore the sun's warmth throughout life, missing out on its spiritual and life enhancing benefits. It's for this reason that I am writing this book, to educate how simply feeling this connection and enjoying its benefits is part of the transformative process of creating a sustainable future. And for this, we can not ignore something as free and obvious as the sun.

If we align ourselves with it, the sun will stop being an annoying blinding light in the sky, causing unbearable heat, forcing us to hide in the shade, and close ourselves in our houses.

Instead, the sun will become the most intriguing phenomenon, the most mysterious object in the sky, virtually a god that you can feel on your skin and also gives you life, as it already does. And then You will bathe in its nourishing, eternal radiance, its liberating burning infinity.

People living in the cloudy parts of the world appreciate the sun and they go out whenever they have nice weather outside. The mood of the population correlates with cloudy or snowy areas. The sun and light are the most obvious mood influencers.

We have even organised our lives around a day-night sleeping schedule. We are biologically wired to wake up with the sun and to sleep during the night.

But we have increasingly arranged our lives to live under artificial light, making us forget the importance of natural light and how it is not separate from the light we are and carry inside.

I have often found myself transfixed gazing at the sunrise or sunset, blown away by its eternally emanating light, which is forever alive just like the shine of our illuminating soul on fire.

The timeless Being is the Sun eternal,
streaming ceaselessly as Awareness,
flowing effortlessly as Abidance.
It is the present kind-heartedness and
a flourishing beauty of the One Beloved

I love the idea that we don't need food and that we can get all the energy we need directly from the sun. This idea, this vision, is as close to freedom as we could get on this planet.

Just imagine being free from having to secure food. We wouldn't need agriculture or any other food production. We wouldn't have to keep and kill animals for meat consumption.

We would end huge karmic damage to the earth and ourselves. We would live free in nature, blessed by the sun.

Ohh, our Sun, the life-giving light!

The very fact that we are self-aware is proof of our energetic nature and gives us a chance in this reality to live by light alone.

The standard practice of sungazing includes a gradual increase of directly looking at the sunrise or sunset until we reach the maximum exposure of thirty minutes. Any longer than that is harmful to the naked eye. The best way to do this practice is in open nature, such as at a beach, field, or hilltop. While gazing at the sun, preferably barefoot, we can practice mindfulness meditation to heighten and fully reap the healing benefits of this illuminating concentration on the sun's light energy.

And of course, in case you were wondering, this has been proven time and time again by the mystics, yogis, and Buddhists who went through scientific testing and confirmed that they haven't eaten or consumed liquids for extended periods. And some of them claim to have been free from food for a lifetime. This ability and technique are like a relic from the ancient past that still finds its way into the modern world. But today only a few are interested or even aware of this possibility since people have been living in a materialistic way of life for so long.

There are, however, many other ancient practices aside from sun gazing still in wide use that are becoming ever so popular. Surya Kriya, for example, activates the sun energy in your body, having a holistic beneficial effect on your well-being as with any other yoga technique. To name a few more, there is the Sun Salutation or Surya Namaskar, then Sun yoga, Lunar yoga, and Sun meditation.

With these you will discover freedom in the sunshine like no other experience could give you. And you will feel and know what I'm talking about once you let go of worldly attachments and of yourself to experience the raw reality of the natural world.

This is a universal certainty as other beings in the universe are looking at the other similar suns and wonder...

IS THE SUN CONSCIOUS?

The idea that matter is conscious, or that everything has consciousness, even matter at least to some degree, is called Panpsychism.

I will stay open to the possibility that in some, I must say miraculous way, the sun as a huge object of mass may have some personal, inner experience, of burning, for example.

If we, such small creatures, have such a rich inner experience of self-awareness, then the massive sun could certainly have some such sense too. It is all part of the one consciousness experiencing itself throughout the entire universe.

Furthermore, as we know that our identity is an illusion, that we are one consciousness having all these universal experiences, every atom and object of mass is therefore somehow also experienced within that one consciousness.

There is a sun burning in every human heart that we can light up, that is, illuminate it with the light of one's authentic undisturbed awareness.

Connection with the sun will extend your consciousness to its natural roots throughout the universe. It will make you free and aware of existence. Any link in the play of life can do that if you see it for what it is, without personal interpretation or ego.

ASTROLOGY

We have named the planets after the Greek and Roman gods, who attributed them with specific personalities. Ancients often depicted the planets, sun, and moon with faces.

And as we have already explored, it is obvious that they saw them as living beings and gods, who were essential for the creation of the universe and life on earth.

All these heavenly bodies assert a strong influence on our culture and behaviour, whether symbolically or physically. This apparently happens through gravitational pull and electromagnetic fields, which impact our brains, hormones, and mood. But as far as they knew in the past, planets were lights in the sky, so their biggest influence was on the spiritual level.

The zodiac is as ancient as humanity, and although there is a definite similarity between the zodiac signs and the sun's influence, we are yet to discover the true mechanics behind such solar energies. I can relate to being an empath, and this is the main characteristic of the cancer sign under which I was born.

I can not say what is causing these inner feelings and sensitivity to the world and people, but whether it is the planets, the sun, or seasons of the year, the emotional side of cancers is undeniable.

As the sun is the largest, heaviest, and gravitationally strong heavenly body affecting the earth, together with the moon, it is the most responsible for any influence on humans too.

There are some reports that the moon emits cold light, as temperatures are colder under the moonlight. Furthermore, the coincidence that the moon and sun have the same size disc in the sky and that we can never see the dark side of the moon is too large to be natural, so the mystery of the moon's origin and role remains.

SPIRITUAL BEING

What does it mean to be a spiritual being? Being aligned with your transcended nature, being aware, being here.

We are beings of pure consciousness, it's our constant unstrippable state, this is who and what we are and it's an undeniable, natural fact. If we don't wake up to this of our own free will, the universe will eventually get us there by another means.

But the power and pull of self-awareness are irresistible, so the more aware you become, the more spiritual you will begin to feel, thus enthusing you to embark on your conscious path of awakening until you melt back into the light.

This can be compared with the growing up process. Once you leave kindergarten, and your childhood passes, you don't regress to playing with toys again, you continue progressing through society and the system, through the social structure until death.

The true awakening is about seeing reality as it is, there is really nothing spiritual about it, rather, raw and natural. But since we live in a materialistic-centred society, we use the term 'spiritual' to describe the opposite of material. And spiritual would then imply knowing, behaving, and acting from the egoless state, which is your natural state of being, one that precedes thought or opinion.

We call that state enlightenment, and everyone is bound to awaken, that is, return to such a state sooner or later, as it is everyone's true and natural state.

Our growing-up process is like a pendulum swinging from side to side, destined to lose energy and remain motionless in place eventually, thus seeing the true state of the universe, one absent of movement of thought.

In light of this observation, some say you can not do anything about enlightenment, it will manifest of its own accord. Or you could speed up the awakening by intensifying the practice of being present, in whatever way feels right at the time.

The idea of time, separation, and individuality are the greatest obstacles to awakening. Meditation and stillness will remember you to reestablish yourself as the power of presence which is the basis for inner peace.

Most people start meditating, changing their diet to vegetarian, vegan, or raw. They orient their time around spiritual studies, interact with a spiritual community, and even join a commune, often trying to live off-grid, free of the system which doesn't fit with the new-found freedom from chasing happiness and success.

They spend most of the time invested in their own being, just being silent, aware, and still. Or, they partake in the most socially rewarding service, such as volunteering work, helping other beings have a chance to live happily by securing their basic human needs.

For this reason, of unconditional giving and caring epitomise unconditional love. Jesus said that the greatest gesture of love is to give your life for another being. We witnessed such love in him, as in all other beings who offer their lives in service to family, friends, community, nation, the animal world, nature, and for civilisation.

Spirituality comes from inside. It is an honouring of your conscious essence. Therefore it can't be a matter of faith, hope, or devotion, for those are religious feelings that come from a belief that a god, or anything at all is physically outside of you.

And yes, there are beings out there in the universe, and we can relate or communicate with them, but this need again comes from your inability to sit peacefully with your own being, which is already complete, to find all the answers within you in the self-awareness.

In doing so, you will of course realise that the questions themselves are the product of an unsettled mind, so you won't need any answers once you abide and dedicate yourself to the inner shrine of peace.

This is non-duality, as opposed to religion and spiritualism, while spirituality would be the simple awareness of being.

We don't even need to call such natural self-awareness spirituality but mere perceiving of raw reality, non-duality. That is a simple shift from out to in, from outer to inner, from out there to here, from past and future to now, from believing in gods to knowing your own being.

This is not some philosophical statement

or New Age idea, it is the only scientific experimental truth that we can ever really know, the only possible truth of who we are as conscious beings. Herein lies the only true joy, one of your most authentic natural being.

Imagine how much energy you can save with this simple shift in awareness. How much of a peaceful place the world would be if we acted in accordance with that inner peace? We certainly wouldn't have religions, national self-identity, pride, or power struggles that lead to wars and the abuse of humanity through a monetary system that creates scarcity on the otherwise abundant earth.

Without wars, we would use technology for sustainable progress only. If we are going to survive the coming decades and secure civilisations' survival for centuries still to come, how can it feasibly be any other way?

We have to work hard to bridge the gap between small-mindedness and open-heartedness. To free ourselves from religious dogma, spiritual superstition, and materialistic ego, finding liberation in the non-dual understanding of reality and of ourselves, which is the raw reality itself.

Thus we can dedicate ourselves to useful values, ones not separate from the sustainable life that we want to create.

Such natural moral inclinations are already inside of us to be cultivated if we don't resist the presence that IS.

To be conscious implies spirituality; to be spiritual means you are connected to the universal nature that you are experiencing here on earth.

To be an experiencer, means you are a being of transcending perception and self-realisation.

All these aspects correspond with the behaviour of light, which is the medium in which consciousness manifests and exists in recognition of itself.

I have not only been looking
into the abyss
I was looking back from
oblivion too

And from tHere
where one day seems
like a lifetime on earth
I have undergone the mystery
as big as the universe's
large scale structure
and greater

A fabric so vast in its complexity
that it would take the computation
of a quantum computer the size
of a super nova to decode it
or God's divine understanding
to comprehend its immensity

An infinite tapestry for
our soul senses

Life

Now some have called it sacred
and some have called it holy
for in the absence of the fear
in the presence of the self
there is a truth that knows divine

Through permeating light of the sunshine
through an open heart of the one
in its flower petal lotus
lies the sweet secret freedom
that rests in a humbling abode

It then flourishes in its generosity
and it does it fully and wholeheartedly
for in seeing, understanding, letting go, and
accepting, it knows the state of the world

In this inner shrine of wisdom
a universal truth of light
the love that the world withholds
is opening up for everyone to know
and feel it as the Joy of Your Being

of JOY

(you are!)

INVITATION

The only true joy is the JOY of your natural being. All else is a fluctuation caused by outside sources. Our purpose in life is to bring about this joy through an awakening from our conditioned happiness or suffering, and we do that by remembering who we are.

Joy is synonymous with inner peace. They are inseparable, the two faces of an enlightened being. But even though peace is our more basic and eternal state as pure consciousness, in this chapter, we will focus on the joy side of the two as it has greater significance and is more appreciated in the world.

Joy arises naturally when we are free from ego, fear, desire, or possessions, provided we don't attach ourselves to it. Such a freed state is then associated with unconditional love, as in the absence of fear and ego; it is where love, peace, and joy are naturally present.
Joy is love, is peace, and is natural smiling.

All of these states could be called the bliss of being. They are natural, meaning we can not fake them and can not hide behind them.

We can, however, induce them artificially for a short period, using substances and experiences, but those do not last.

Throughout history, we had the privilege of knowing certain beings whose states of joy are lasting and are independent of outside circumstances. We call them mystics or sages.

By observing themselves over long periods, their state of joy, or absorption in the bliss of being, in the self, was self-evident.

Of course, many people desire the same joy, to reciprocate such a state, so we ask them to teach us by explaining their state and sharing the secret of happiness. The result is numerous spiritual paths and techniques, religions, and movements. So after a few millennia, we now have a vast collection of knowledge, but correspondingly, we were never so captivated or confused by it.

That is the main reason for writing this book, to dilute many practices and focus on the one eternal truth of being, the JOY of BEING YOU.

WHAT IS THE JOY?

The joy is who you are, in essence. Uncluttered by the incessant activity of the mind, which obscures your natural being and experiences itself as a separate identity. That is the root of feeling incomplete, of missing your essential nature as awareness. This simple misunderstanding is the main reason for losing our inherent presence that creates the world of unconsciousness from which we are trying to awaken.

We, however, mostly end up in a trap of chasing happiness. As kids, we only want to play and have fun. In adolescence, we look for satisfaction in relationships, sports, or substances. As adults, we seek the security of a family, a job, and retirement. Society seems hardwired to the premise of feeling good by enjoying goods, activities, and social interactions.

But do we ever take our heads out of the sand of comfort and see the natural state of things? Do we ever ask if is there a more basic or easier way to live, to be happy, to be joyous?

The answer is as simple yet profound and shocking as anyone can imagine!

As you may suspect, the answer is the opposite of what society has taught us.

You are already happy and are born to experience this joy of being and fulfilment with life that we have chased for so long throughout human civilisation. You are the happiness you seek in the world. You are the joy of who you always wanted and are trying to be.

This realisation is so life-changing that we call it Awakening or Enlightenment. However, we have associated these what appear to be imaginary states of bliss with only the spiritual greats such as Buddha, Jesus, and Ramana.

We see many people being happy in their lives, but are they truly conscious of themselves or just indulging in satisfying their character roles? For them, ignorance truly is bliss. To be fully self-conscious and abide in joy, we need to dig ourselves up from the mud of ego and intellectual prowess. We need to hit upon that one liberating insight of the natural inner power; we are already free from the world.

By that, I mean freedom from whatever prevents us from experiencing our true potential as beings of joy. We are held back by the deeply ingrained beliefs that we are separate from others, from the world, that we are individual beings with minds of our own, and the perception that the world is outside our point of attention. And finally, the corresponding experiences of having thoughts, feelings, and sensations while interacting with such a world compound this. But this world and our sense of individuality prove to be a mental construct of the human brain. And although we can not deny our awareness, the experienced duality is imaginary.

So the question now is: are we really happy or is our happiness the result of a constant satisfying of needs? When those needs are not met, we suffer. Have we arranged our lives in such a way as to hide this dilemma, never speaking aloud about such depths of life? Have we become so ashamed of ourselves, our natural curiosity, and our basic needs that it has come to the point of ignoring and hiding them from ourselves, the masses, and our children?

Our lives certainly do seem to be prearranged, starting with preschool education leading to primary education, to high school, college, job, marriage, career, and retirement. Our vision stops there. We don't even talk about death. We don't talk about anything that is the basis of human life. Rather, we ignore it with stereotypical behaviour and even have a tendency to ridicule the individuals who raise these naturally curious issues.

Such overlooking of basic life questions is our troubled human condition. It is the system, the status quo, the big brother, the matrix. We are afraid of losing our safety, and our comfort in society if we ask the big questions, such as the base question of whether I am truly happy or is my life a rollercoaster of chasing the surface pleasures and obeying the Man.

Consequently, life passes in an instant and we find ourselves on our deathbeds thinking, have I wasted my whole life, have I ever been truly free? Have I ever known or experienced true joy?

And we know from the people who are dying that the first regret they have is not having the courage to live the life of their dreams, or simply to be themselves. Even the simple but painful inability to say to the people close to us that we love them. We carry a heavy burden of pain and regret by delaying living with an open heart, missing out on our life purpose, which simultaneously contributes to the general unconsciousness of the world.

How do we heal ourselves and save the

world? We free ourselves from ourselves, that is, our problems, by letting go of them as we sense and internalise our natural joy of being.

HOW TO AWAKEN THE JOY?

Our natural joy is already here, shining ever so brightly and infinitely. It corresponds with the consciousness in which everything exists. As long as we remain abiding in its eternal presence, we will be the beings of joy, just as we were born, as children with their innate, natural ability to smile and be happy.

You don't have to create or accomplish anything to be joyous, understanding that is the core realisation. Joy, peace, or consciousness can be described as the shining light of the sun, it is always tHere. Our problems are the clouds that cover joy and overshadow our will to live. We don't have to create joy, as it is already alive inside of us. We only need to see the illusion of the cloud formations, how thoughts about the past or future pull us from the present moment where our natural being resides.

It's not the thoughts themselves that are the problem, it's identifying with them, giving us the feeling the experience is happening to us, which is the problem. This simple misidentification is the result of our materialistic upbringing that causes us to take everything personally.

But the joy is general, and it is free, vividly emanating from our open hearts. With it, we can deeply appreciate the miracle of being alive, settling us in graceful peace. And peace implies being at ease with the present moment.

No matter the situation, peace is always an underlying structure of interactions. Whatever we do or say, we are coming out of peace, out of silence, and we will inevitably return to it. These qualities of being conscious are interrelated. Consciousness allows for existence; silence breathes peace; love awakens joy; aliveness brings about bliss.

Peoples' first glimpses of joy are often through the use of substances and satisfying hedonistic pleasures. That creates an addictive or habitual need for a lifelong relationship with such providers of happiness, which is not an authentic, free, natural joy of being.

We end up addicted to smoking; consuming coffee, alcohol, and meat; stuck in relationships primarily based on social and sexual status and satisfaction rather than on one's soul essence.

A different taste of joy or completion comes from the religious experience of surrender, the belief that God takes care of all our problems. People derive tremendous power and inspiration from such faithful relaxation and freedom from themselves.

And this joy is closer to home, as it is rooted in spiritual ideology and the most authentic feelings of love and peace. We could say that Buddhists are the closest to the religious path to joy. Instead of attaching themselves to deities, they appreciate their teacher's inspiration as well as practicing concentrating deeply on the present moment.

Non-dual advocates are, however,
at the true home, as there is no attachment
whatsoever, only paying complete attention
to their own being.

Ramana Maharshi is probably the most
well-known embodiment of such freedom
in life. He was a fully self-realised being.

And if you haven't yet allowed yourself to
melt in his graceful gaze of eternal warmth
and blissful presence, you have the most
beautiful chance to do so.

Maybe start with the famous
documentary on his life and teachings
The Sage of Arunachala, which I find to
be the most spiritually inspiring.

Also, *The Little Buddha* with Keanu Reeves plus any of those old Jesus movies can truly bring you closer to your true self by stripping you of the fear to show you how infinite love acts on earth. They are larger than life, and their influence is far-reaching.

But until we realise the right symbiosis relating to our true self and nature, until we have a definitive line that we cannot cross, we will be drawn to over-reach our living capacities, which is not conducive to achieving any sustainable reality.

The only way to stay sane is to live in the countryside and grow your own food. Everything else is dead consumerism, useless, and wasteful globalism.

The only reason you enjoy being separate is your ego. That illusory feeling of I, me, mine is the root of all evil, the base of all separation.

Isolation is the main source of all the problems in this world. You isolate yourself in your houses and raise yourself individually, ignoring the rest of society, under the illusion of private living.

But imagine if you were constantly surrounded by hundreds of people, you would always work for the benefit of the entire community. There wouldn't be rich or poor neighbours, everyone would develop collectively.

There would be no stress, fear, competition, lack, jealousy, divorce, the burden of raising children alone, the monetary pressure, I mean there would be no problems whatsoever.

Every true teacher has lived in communion, with others, never isolated, never alone within the confounds of any walls, but freely walking in nature.

So imagine being free in nature, living in a wooden house with an open terrace, facing a garden and landscape views.

Also envision a future world where there is no longer money or real jobs, where everything is free, where everybody socialises openly, and we all contribute to the needs of society. It is a utopia where you freely work on your hobbies and skills and then you can share them with the world.

Fresh organic food would be everywhere in every neighbourhood, we would all use public bicycles, cars, and vehicles; everything required is for free.

It is the perfect world where entire humanity is one big family.

We need to allow and facilitate such a world with our inner peace and compassion. So many people suffer, yet the greatest love is in helping others.

ABSENCE OF THOUGHTS

God is your awareness of breath, the absence of thought. He is unnamable but knowable; he is the knowing. He is unapproachable but present; he is the presence. He is untouchable but felt; he is a feeling of being. He is unmovable but everywhere; he is beingness.

God can not be found out there; he is always here. It can not be met but recognised as the inner home of stillness. God is isness that IS. Presentness; the absence of thoughts.

It can be in your darkest hour that he makes himself known to you, as the knowing of your being, as knowing, as being, in the space of no time, as nowness.

Spirituality of the joy of being is not something you force or even practice; it is who you are when settled in stillness, in breath awareness.

Wake up with ease, stay present, and be thankful to existence for clarity and health. Drink only water to start the day and meditate for breakfast. The awesome feeling of goodness

will vibrate through your cells. After you take a walk in the natural ambiance of your environment, eat some light fruits that make your soul flourish on the energy of their freshness. Fully energised, you are ready for the day of communal service, and to engage with your fellow community of soul workers whose days are as bright as the light,
call them lightworkers.

You now have a master plan to dedicate your time to the others who are trapped in the grip of adhering to thoughts, bound to chase happiness in addictive pleasures, unable to observe themselves, lost in the game,
the drama, and the thrill of a chase.

But you stay as the bright sunshine, invigorated by the inner pleasantness of stillness; present and still, knowing, being.

Here are a few ways you can drastically progress in your conscious life and
awaken your natural joy:

— Routine schedule:
Go to sleep early and wake up early.
Start your day healthily, with no mobile phone,

just be with yourself, meditate, stretch,
have a refreshing breakfast, read,
and work on projects.

— Drop the adictive social media:
Stop all the popular music, television shows,
and all teenage entertainment. Dedicate time
only to professional adult behaviour, quality
people and conversations. Consume a healthy
social-media diet. Invest all spare time into
career progression, studies, college, courses,
training, learning, and events.

— Your inner spirit matters the most:
Spirituality, meditation, outdoors, nature, love.
Travel, take cold shower, fast, sungaze, love.
Be fully conscious of yourself, always. LOVE!

— Be genuine:
Always tell the truth and maintain close social
interactions, work on what you love and like,
enjoy your day fully immersed in creativity
and pursuits that awaken your life's purpose.

— Relaxing evening:
Again no junk-funs, just be in peace, read,

eat a light dinner, dedicate time to yourself,
ensure peace is completely within you,
go to sleep early with no devices, no
obstructions, and nothing to think about for
an overall inner quality of being present.

I send you my loving energy in honour
of all the pain which has caused us to awaken
and realise we are love and have always
been loved.
You are loved with every breath you take,
every tear you've cried, every moment you've
appreciated. You are eternally and forever
loved by the universe, by me; we are love!
I Love You!

We exist to return to this healing oneness,
and our combined energies are the point of
this blessing of thankfulness for conscious life.

**You are the beauty of a pure being
embracing the world as the soul's sol**

witnessing the miracles of existence

**refreshing the seamless desire of
becoming one and whole again**

SUNSHINE

Once again, let's return to our main theme
and inspiration for this book and my favourite
natural sensation: when I close my eyes and
stand in front of the sun, looking and feeling
those warm colours of orange, yellow, and red,
playing like a plasma dance of energy, here,
I feel at home. I don't need anything else other
than that sensation of illuminating radiance.

For me, this is the best feeling ever.
It is like the true vision of our conscious
pure life energy, which holds an entire
potential for manifestation, creation,
and design within itself.

**Close your eyes in front of
the healing rays of sunshine**

To bathe in this emulation of soul-energy food is the height of self-recognition as a deathless spirit. That is the feeling with which I want to associate my spiritual investments, my hopes, and dreams of eternity.

Total darkness is one extreme, sunshine is the other. Maybe there is no middle way here, it is the combination of the two, the yin yang interplay of darkness and light, of coldness and heat, both equally beautiful, both equivalently terrifying.

Sun is our god, we are its sons. But this is not about some ancient or pagan worship, it is about recognition of the natural order of things. Seeing, feeling, and acting in a realistic way in correspondence with the raw reality of the universe, solar system, earth, and environment.

So we can symbolically and literally say that the sun is our god, and nature our home. Spirituality is about seeing and feeling the deeper aspects of that raw reality, which initially appears to be only material.

Allowing it to freely vibrate inside your

heart is what it truly means to be alive,
this is the Being of Joy.

All these aspects of existence as
conscious beings are interrelated and need to
be understood, as well as openly perceived.

Finally, you will walk in the ecstasy of
stillness, perfect attention, and
inevitable joy which follow.

PRESENCE

THere exists one permeating, undeniable
reality of your own conscious being. Its
perception is free, where the moment is full
of itselfness. Its vision is the sun's light, its life
the heart of being. Its time in place is localised,
but its space is infinite and now.

It is in the perfect moment of stillness, that
you will know it until it disappears again with
the world of movement. But it is never lost, it
patiently observes the passing of all risings.
And then it finds itself again in the presence
of its presence, in the knowing of its being.

Yes, it can act, play, do, perform, get lost,
marry, raise children, and accomplish a career,

but it knows that the moment of final recognition will arrive, as it knows that it has been and is always here.

Death could reunite it with the one, only for it to start searching once again for itself in the world, the movement, in the stillness.

THere is nothing more powerful in this world and existence than your own light of presence. The light here is the love of your soul. The presence is your unperishable consciousness; the present awareness.

And upon enquiring closely, there it notices, it knows, it is the only thing that exists at all. You exist within it, and it can not stop existing. It can not stop being. You can not disappear, die, or cease to be.

What you can do, the only thing you can ever do, is to be with its being, to be the being. For this reason, you don't have to practice so-called awakening, but only release yourself into the being which is already here, which already and always was and will be you.

Don't even try to let go of anything, which immediately implies holding on to something, rather, notice the presentness of your own

calm being. Be present, be still, and allow
the thoughts to naturally settle. Be observant,
be observance, be free within that space of
presentness. Be awaring, noticing, looking,
knowing, and being. Remain aware.

In such calming of the body and mind, you
are finally alive. Now you know yourself fully,
and in knowing yourself you know the world
and everybody else in it. You know existence
because you are existing and knowing
yourself as That.

You are being, and you know yourself
as beingness. You are aware and you know
yourself as the awareness. You are present
and know yourself as a presence.

And in so doing you are still as stillness,
calm as calmness. You are bright as
the light of knowing.

Thus, you are awake as you are awakening,
and you are enlightened as you are light
as the light itself.

The ground and walls, seem dense and
heavy as matter, but you see through it as you
float freely in the sea of open space as the
consciousness that you are.

You don't have to know all the inner workings of the universe, the explanatory laws of movement and vibration, you are enough simply by being present. That is your blessing, your secret, your freedom, and your joy in this life as a self-aware being of light.

There is no other knowledge than knowing yourself as an awareness, and no other action or doing needed other than pure being.

That is what you can not escape from, as it is the gift of existence to know and recognise itself through your conscious self.

Align yourself with the presence of your own awareness and you will be at peace. You will be the joy of being you, the being of joy, the joy that is being. You are it. Be.

THE NEW EARTH

Right now, and for millennia already, humanity is living in the egoic state of consciousness, or unconsciousness.

This type of perception is responsible for the dog-eat-dog way of life, where we are still slaves to a monetary system, and most people suffer to survive. Of course, the past was even worse times basically without workers' rights or even jobs as such. So we can say that we are progressing, but it is too slow and with devastating consequences for the environment as well as the human mentality and spirit. We have now reached the point where it is unclear whether our civilisation will even survive the coming decade.

Life is out there, in cities, nature, places, and with people. It is not in our houses, living rooms, and bedrooms. How much of your life do you remember spending in the house, and how much being adventurous? We are all too accustomed to working and being at home, but this is a deadly routine and far from living authentically, call it wild and free.

Humans are being educated or indoctrinated to fit into the working class, to not become conscious of the bigger picture or themselves at all.

Humanity needs to be educated in a way where every individual will legitimately become fully self-aware. One will learn the value of the soil, water, animals, and plant life.

But above all, the absolute necessity of working together as one civilisation to secure a sustainable present for an abundant future.

Do you want to live in anything else, with anything less? If we are not doing our part in this evolution of conscious education, then we are collectively wasting precious time to start healing the earth.

And I promise you it will be a beautiful world, almost too fantastic in appearance and too futuristic to comprehend, but it is one we are destined to organise and create. It will be a quieter world, adorned with vegetation.

Forests will be everywhere, with the magnificent wildlife keeping the flora and fauna original, useful, and alive. You will feel the force of the pure and natural energy of life. Above all, you will be free from work slavery and will work freely of your free will to keep this fascinating, sustainable civilisation going.

Then, we will be worthy of calling ourselves the human civilisation. We will be fulfilling our highest potential, the humanity of miracles. The race of space explorations, aiming for the highest self, the best, healthiest, and most knowledgeable. And correspondingly, acting from the highest self, finding the best solutions, producing the healthiest food, and exploring our understanding of universal existence.

But finally, first and foremost, knowing the Self.

We thus have to turn astrology into astronomy, religion into science, and ignorance into knowledge.

One thing is certain, this new better world will not function without you. You are as significant as the entire civilised structure. Every individual is of utmost importance and has a lasting influence on the longevity of such a world. It will belong to everyone, not just a safe haven exclusively for the selected few.

That is the reason we exist as a civilisation, it is the purpose of our lives. We are the chosen generation that is already bringing this dream into tangible reality as the old outdated social and economic order is collapsing, taking the tyranny of democracies and communism with it. We don't follow these anymore, we lead ourselves by our highest selves.

That shining liberation of human potential and spirit that has so far been neglected and sleeping, is dreaming of awakening to enable the raw reality of the natural world, to finally flourish and manifest our enlightened dreams.

To be a part of this transformation is a calling of utmost joy. Returning to yourself as a being of joy, in a happy world, with a joyful heart.

Celebrate your uniqueness by sharing your gifts of the soul with the global community, contributing to the general well-being of humanity. Be absolutely free in expressing your particular standpoint.

You are one original, real expression of the universe that is made conscious through your body's energy field and your mind's mental capacity to integrate your living being.

So let us unite in this cause for perseverance. Let us awaken the courage to tap into the source of life essence that freely vibrates in each of our hearts. This universal calling is pulsating and steering the cosmic impulse of your soul to break through the mind-

dominated self and bring forth
our destined sustainable livelihood.

Well, come on then,
there is no time left to lose,
what option is there but to focus and
engage all our sacred intelligence on
transmuting unconsciousness into
a golden dawn...

The sunrise of Awakening

The sunset of Illumination

Petar Umiljanović,

was born in Croatia on the 28th of June 1987.

From an early age, He felt strangely connected to and interested in the Universe, Nature, Religion, and Mysteries, along with Science, History, Ufology, Sport, and Music.

Later, profound insights into Psychology, Philosophy, and Spirituality led Him to investigate the True nature of the Self, revealing Consciousness as the only constant Presence.

Upon moving to Ireland and travelling Europe, thus engaging in many arts and activities, especially experiencing a deep relationship with Nature, this book was gradually inspired.

Contact:
petarumiljanovic@gmail.com

NOTES

NOTES